INSIGHTS
Miracles

INSIGHTS

Miracles

What the Bible Tells Us about Jesus' Miracles

WILLIAM BARCLAY

SAINT ANDREW PRESS
Edinburgh

First published in 2011 by
SAINT ANDREW PRESS
121 George Street
Edinburgh EH2 4YN

Copyright © The William Barclay Estate 1975, 2001
Layout copyright © Saint Andrew Press, 2011

ISBN 978 0 7152 0933 2

British Library Cataloguing in Publication Data
A catalogue record for this book is available from the British Library.

It is the publisher's policy to only use papers that are natural and
recyclable and that have been manufactured from timber grown
in renewable, properly managed forests. All of the manufacturing
processes of the papers are expected to conform to the environmental
regulations of the country of origin.

Typeset by Waverley Typesetters, Warham, Norfolk
Printed and bound by Bell & Bain Ltd, Glasgow

Contents

Foreword

I grew up, in a sense, with William Barclay. His name was quoted many times in the house groups my parents ran; I heard it from the pulpits under which I sat through childhood years. His was a name spoken with reverence and honour; I remember a whole shelf of his books in my father's study.

But it's only now, through reading this work of his on the miracles of Jesus, that I've come to understand why William Barclay's name has been so revered, and why he is respected as such a great teacher and broadcaster.

The gospel accounts give us just a few words to work with; it's all too easy to read the miracles, accept them, pass on. Barclay has a breathtakingly rich knowledge of the world in which the gospel is set; he knows about the flow of a certain river, the precise naming of a particular place. The little nuggets of insight; the wise commentary on the Greek. The different perspectives within the community of Jesus' time; the cultural context of events. He is a contemporary man moving easily and efficiently in a New Testament landscape.

But at no point does he wear that knowledge heavily, over-conscious of his own skill. On the contrary, he is one of us – looking to learn more. Nor is he so obsessed by this New Testament landscape that he neglects his own time: the stories of contemporary writers and scholars are deftly woven into the fabric of the text. The weaving is done in such a way that the reader never loses interest; we are drawn on instead, to the next point and the next, never bogged down in a tangle of theological heather roots.

The intention is to give us a full sense of the power of Jesus' miracles. Often that means widening our perspective, getting us to see the whole breadth of the miracle's consequences, beyond the narrow bit we thought we always knew. So often he picks up on what we pass over.

Most of all he wants to leave us with the clear message that miracles did not stop at the end of Jesus' ministry on earth. The final sentence of the book makes that abundantly clear: *For Christians there are still miracles all around if they have eyes to see.*

KENNETH STEVEN

Publisher's Introduction

Perhaps the most famous of Jesus' miracles is the story of the loaves and the fishes. Jesus, as we all know, took a young lad's five loaves and two fishes and somehow fed a large crowd. It is a favourite childhood story, confirming to the young listener the great power of Jesus. But there are subtler messages for adults, if we care to look for them.

William Barclay's great skill in communicating the New Testament was based on his belief that the Scriptures should be made clear by using ordinary language and by setting them in context. So, in this story – the loaves and the fishes – Barclay points out that Jesus was under continuous strain and needed to rest. He needed to find time for prayer, away from the authorities who were trying to find a way to have him arrested. This is the political context. We learn that the route taken by Jesus across the Sea of Galilee was four miles long, and that a crowd of people, fascinated by his words and actions, followed him by land across the River Jordan on a nine-mile route. This is the geographical context. Their numbers were swollen by a crowd of pilgrims on their way to celebrate the Feast of the Passover, who had taken a long route to avoid the hated Samaritans. This is the religious context.

Barclay also gives fascinating information on the food, the customs, the people and much else besides: things that would have been known 2,000 years ago in the middle east, but not so well known to us today. The detail allows us to understand the story as it was meant to be understood.

Then he goes on to explain the miracle itself. Perhaps the miracle was just that: a miraculous event beyond our understanding. Or maybe it was a sacramental meal, so that each person received but a morsel. 'In the rest of the chapter,' writes Barclay, 'the language of Jesus is exactly that of the Last Supper, when he speaks about eating his flesh and drinking his blood.' Or perhaps, according to Barclay, there was another 'very lovely' explanation. We won't reveal that explanation here: you can read it in the first section of this book.

As always with Barclay, there are lessons for us to learn: an old, very familiar story has very real meaning for us all today. By adding the context to a short passage, Barclay inspires people to return with renewed confidence and enthusiasm to the Scriptures.

You can read more about the context of the miracles in the following New Daily Study Bibles: *Matthew 1* and *Matthew 2*; *Mark*; *Luke*, *John 1* and *John 2*; and Acts of the Apostles. All of these books, and the rest of the series, are available from Saint Andrew Press.

The loaves and fishes

After these things Jesus went away across the Sea of Galilee, that is, the Sea of Tiberias. A great crowd was following him, because they were watching the signs which he did on those who were ill. Jesus went up into the hill and he was sitting there with his disciples. The Passover, the Feast of the Jews, was near. When Jesus lifted up his eyes and saw that a great crowd was coming to him, he said to Philip: 'Where are we to buy bread for these to eat?' He was testing Philip when he said this, for he himself knew what he was going to do. Philip answered him: 'Even 200 denarii worth of bread is not enough to give each of them a little to eat.' One of the disciples said to him – it was Andrew, Simon Peter's brother – 'There is a lad here who has five barley loaves and two little fishes. But what use are they among so many?' Jesus said: 'Make the men sit down.' There was much grass in the place. So the men sat down to the number of about 5,000. So Jesus took the loaves and gave thanks for them, and divided them up among those who were reclining there. So too he gave them of the fishes, as much as they wished. When they were satisfied, he said to the disciples: 'Collect the broken pieces that are left over, so that nothing may be wasted.' So they collected them, and they filled twelve baskets with the broken pieces of the loaves which remained over after the people had eaten.

THERE were times when Jesus desired to withdraw from the crowds. He was under continuous strain and needed rest. Moreover, it was necessary that sometimes he should get his disciples alone to lead them into a deeper understanding of himself. In addition, he needed time for prayer. On this particular occasion, it was wise to go away before a head-on collision with the authorities took place, for the time of the final conflict had not yet come.

From Capernaum to the other side of the Sea of Galilee was a distance of about four miles, and Jesus set sail. The people had been watching with astonishment the things he did; it was easy to see the direction the boat was taking; and they hastened round the top of the lake by land. The River Jordan flows into the north end of the Sea of Galilee. Two miles up the river were the fords of Jordan. Near the fords was a village called Bethsaida Julias, to distinguish it from the other Bethsaida in Galilee, and it was for that place that Jesus was making (Luke 9:10). Near Bethsaida Julias, almost on the lakeside, was a little plain where the grass always grew. It was to be the scene of a wondrous happening.

At first, Jesus went up into the hill behind the plain and he was sitting there with his disciples. Then the crowd began to appear in droves. It was nine miles round the top of the lake and across the ford, and they had made the journey with all speed. We are told that the Feast of the Passover was near and there would be even bigger crowds on the roads at that time. Possibly many were on the way to Jerusalem by that route. Many Galilaean pilgrims travelled north and crossed the ford and went through Peraea, and then recrossed the Jordan near Jericho. The way was longer, but it avoided the territory of the hated and dangerous Samaritans. It is likely that the great crowd was swelled by detachments of pilgrims on their way to the Passover Feast.

At the sight of the crowd, Jesus' sympathy was kindled. They were hungry and tired, and they must be fed. Philip was the natural man to whom to turn, for he came from Bethsaida (John 1:44) and would have local knowledge. Jesus asked him where food could be got. Philip's answer was despairing. He said that even if food could be got it would cost more than 200 denarii to give this vast crowd even a little each. A denarius was the standard day's wage for a working man. Philip calculated that it would take more than six months' wages to begin to feed a crowd like this.

Then Andrew appeared on the scene. He had discovered a young boy with five barley loaves and two little fishes. Quite likely the boy had brought them as a picnic lunch. Maybe he was out for the day, and as a boy might, had attached himself to the crowd. Andrew, as usual, was bringing people to Jesus.

The boy had not much to bring. Barley bread was the cheapest of all bread and was held in contempt. There is a regulation in the Mishnah about the offering that a woman who has committed adultery must bring. She must, of course, bring a trespass offering. With all offerings a food offering was made, and the food offering consisted of flour and wine and oil intermixed. Ordinarily the flour used was made of wheat; but it was laid down that, in the case of an offering for adultery, the flour could be barley flour, for barley is the food of animals, and the woman's sin was the sin of an animal. Barley bread was the bread of the very poor.

The fishes would be no bigger than sardines. Pickled fish from Galilee were known all over the Roman Empire.

In those days, fresh fish was an unheard-of luxury, for there was no means of transporting it any distance and keeping it in an eatable condition. Small sardine-like fish swarmed in the Sea of Galilee. They were caught and pickled and made into a kind of savoury. The boy had his little pickled fish to help the dry barley bread down.

Jesus told the disciples to make the people sit down. He took the loaves and the fishes and he blessed them. When he did that, he was acting as father of the family. The grace he used would be the one that was used in every home: 'Blessed art Thou, O Lord, our God, who causest to come forth bread from the earth.' The people ate and were filled. Even the word that is used for *filled* (*chortazesthai*) is suggestive. Originally, in classical Greek, it was a word used for feeding animals with fodder. When used of people, it meant that they were fed to repletion.

When the people had eaten their fill, Jesus bade his disciples gather up the fragments left. Why the fragments? At Jewish feasts, the regular practice was to leave something for the servants. That which was left was called the *Peah*; and no doubt the people left their usual part for those who had served them with the meal.

Of the fragments, twelve baskets were taken up. No doubt each of the disciples had his basket (*kophinos*). It was bottle-shaped, and no Jew ever travelled without one. Twice the Roman satirist Juvenal (3:14, 6:542) talks of 'the Jew with his basket and his truss of hay'. (The truss of hay was to use as a bed, for many of the Jews lived a nomadic life.) The Jew with his basket was a well-recognized figure. He carried it because he needed to carry his own food if he was going to observe the Jewish rules of cleanness and uncleanness. From the fragments, each of the disciples filled his basket. And so the hungry crowd were fed and more than fed.

The meaning of a miracle

WE will never know exactly what happened on that grassy plain near Bethsaida Julias. We may look at it in three ways.

(a) We may regard it simply as a miracle in which Jesus multiplied loaves and fishes. Some may find that hard to conceive of; and some may find it hard to reconcile with the fact that that is just what Jesus refused to do at his temptations (Matthew 4:3–4). If we can believe in the sheer miraculous character of this miracle, then let us continue to do so. But if we are puzzled, there are two other explanations.

(b) It may be that this was really a sacramental meal. In the rest of the chapter, the language of Jesus is exactly that of the Last Supper, when he speaks about eating his flesh and drinking his blood. It could be that at this meal it was but a morsel, like the sacrament, that each person received; and that the thrill and wonder of the presence of Jesus and the reality of God turned the sacramental crumb into something which richly nourished their hearts and souls – as happens at every communion service to this day.

(c) There may be another and very lovely explanation. It is scarcely to be thought that the crowd left on a nine-mile expedition without making any preparations at all. If there were pilgrims with them, they would certainly possess supplies for the way. But it may be that they would not produce what they had, for they selfishly – and very humanly – wished to keep it all for themselves. It may then be that Jesus, with that rare smile of his, produced the little store that he and his disciples had; with sunny faith he thanked God for it and shared it out. Moved by his example, everyone who had anything did the same; and in the end there was enough, and more than enough, for all.

It may be that this is a miracle in which the presence of Jesus turned a crowd of selfish men and women into a fellowship of sharers. It may be that this story represents the biggest miracle of all – one which changed not loaves and fishes, but men and women.

However that may be, there were certain people there without whom the miracle would not have been possible.

(1) There was Andrew. There is a contrast between Andrew and Philip. Philip was the man who said: 'The situation is hopeless; nothing can be done.' Andrew was the man who said: 'I'll see what I can do; and I'll trust Jesus to do the rest.'

It was Andrew who brought that young boy to Jesus, and by bringing him made the miracle possible. No one ever knows what will come out of it when we bring someone to Jesus. If parents train up their children in the knowledge and the love and the fear of God, no one can say what mighty things those children may some day do for God and for others. If a Sunday School teacher brings a child to Christ, no one knows what that child may some day do for Christ and his Church.

There is a tale of an old German schoolmaster who, when he entered his class of boys in the morning, used to remove his cap and bow ceremoniously to them. One asked him why he did this. His answer was: 'You never know what one of these boys may some day become.' He was right – one of them was the founder of the Reformation, Martin Luther.

Andrew did not know what he was doing when he brought that boy to Jesus that day, but he was providing material for a miracle. We never know what possibilities we are releasing when we bring someone to Jesus.

(2) There was the boy. He had not much to offer, but in what he had Jesus found the materials of a miracle. There would have been one great deed fewer in history if that boy had withheld his loaves and fishes.

Jesus needs what we can bring him. It may not be much, but he needs it. It may well be that the world is denied miracle after miracle and triumph after triumph because we will not bring to Jesus what we have and what we are. If we would lay ourselves on the altar of his service, there is no saying what he could do with us and through us. We may be sorry and embarrassed that we have not more to bring – and rightly so; but that is no reason for failing to bring what we have. Little is always much in the hands of Christ.

The leper is cleansed

Mark 1:40–5

> *A leper came to him, asking him to help him and kneeling before him. 'If you are willing to do so,' he said, 'you are able to cleanse me.' Jesus was moved with pity to the depths of his being.*
>
> *He stretched out his hand and touched him. 'I am willing,' Jesus said, 'be cleansed.' Immediately the leprosy left him and he was cleansed. Immediately Jesus sent him away with a stern injunction. 'See to it', he said to him, 'that you tell no man anything about this; but go and show yourself to the priest, and bring the offering for cleansing which Moses laid down, so that you may prove to them that you really are healed.' He went away and began to proclaim the story at length and to spread it all over. The result was that it was not possible for Jesus to come openly into any town, but he had to stay outside in the lonely places; and they kept coming to him from all over.*

In the New Testament there is no disease regarded with more terror and pity than leprosy. When Jesus sent out the Twelve he commanded them, 'Heal the sick, cleanse lepers' (Matthew 10:8). The fate of the leper was truly hard.

Here is one of the most revealing pictures of Jesus.

(1) He did not drive away a man who had broken the law. The leper had no right to have spoken to him at all, but Jesus

met the desperation of human need with an understanding compassion.

(2) Jesus stretched out his hand and touched him. He touched the man who was unclean. To Jesus he was not unclean; he was simply a human soul in desperate need.

(3) Having cleansed him, Jesus sent him to fulfil the prescribed ritual. He fulfilled the human law and human righteousness. He did not recklessly defy the conventions, but, when need be, submitted to them.

Here we see compassion, power and wisdom all at work together.

A faith that would not be denied

Mark 2:1–6

> *When, some time afterwards, Jesus had come back to Capernaum, the news went round that he was in a house. Such crowds collected that there was no longer any room left, not even round the door. So he was speaking the word to them. A party arrived bringing to him a paralysed man carried by four men. When they could not get near him because of the crowd they unroofed part of the roof of the house in which he was, and when they had dug out part of the roof, they let down the stretcher on which the paralysed man was lying. When Jesus saw their faith, he said to the paralysed man, 'Child, your sins are forgiven.'*

AFTER Jesus had completed his tour of the synagogues, he returned to Capernaum. The news of his coming immediately spread abroad. Life in Palestine was very public. In the morning the door of the house was opened and anyone who wished might come out and in. The door was never shut unless someone deliberately wished for privacy; an open door meant an open invitation for all to come in. In the humbler houses, such as this must have been, there was no entrance hall; the door opened directly on to the street. So, in no time, a crowd had filled the house to capacity and jammed the pavement round the door; and they were all eagerly listening to what Jesus had to say.

Into this crowd came four men carrying on a stretcher a friend of theirs who was paralysed. They could not get through the crowd at all, but they were men of resource. The roof of a Palestinian house was flat. It was regularly used as a place of rest and of quiet, and so usually there was an outside stair which ascended to it. The construction of the roof lent itself to what these ingenious four proposed to do. The roof consisted of flat beams laid across from wall to wall, perhaps three feet apart. The space in between the beams was filled with brushwood packed tight with clay. The top was then made watertight. Very largely the roof was of earth and often a flourishing crop of grass grew on the roof of a Palestinian house. It was the easiest thing in the world to dig out the filling between two of the beams; it did not even damage the house very much, and it was easy to repair the breach again. So the four men dug out the filling between two of the beams and let their friend down directly at Jesus' feet. When Jesus saw this faith that laughed at barriers, he must have smiled an understanding smile. He looked at the man, 'Child,' he said, 'your sins are forgiven.'

It may seem an odd way to begin a cure. But in Palestine, in the time of Jesus, it was natural and inevitable. The Jews integrally connected sin and suffering. They argued that if people were suffering they must have sinned. That is in fact the argument that Job's friends produced. 'Who', demanded Eliphaz the Temanite, 'that was innocent ever perished?' (Job 4:7). The Rabbis had a saying, 'There is no sick man healed of his sickness until all his sins have been forgiven him.' To the Jews, a sick person was someone with whom God was angry. It is true that a great many illnesses are due to sin; it is still truer that time and time again they are due not to the sin of the one who is ill, but to the sin of others. We do not make the close connection that the Jews did, but any Jew would have agreed that forgiveness of sins was a prior condition of cure.

It may well be, however, that there is more than this in this story. The Jews made this connection between illness and sin, and it may well be that, in this case, *the man's conscience agreed*. And it may well be that that consciousness of sin had actually produced the paralysis. The power of the mind, especially the subconscious mind, over the body is an amazing thing.

Psychologists quote a case of a girl who played the piano in a cinema in the days of the silent films. Normally she was quite well, but immediately the lights went out and cigarette smoke filled the auditorium she began to be paralysed. She fought against it for a long time, but at last the paralysis became permanent and something had to be done. Examination revealed no physical cause whatever. Under hypnosis it was discovered that when she was very young, only a few weeks old, she had been lying in one of those elaborate old-fashioned cots with an arch of lace over it. Her mother had bent over her smoking a cigarette. The draperies had caught fire. It was immediately extinguished and no physical harm was done to her, but her subconscious mind was remembering this terror. The dark plus the smell of the cigarette smoke in the cinema acted on the unconscious mind and paralysed her body – and she did not know why.

The man in this story may well have been paralysed because consciously or unconsciously his conscience agreed that he was a sinner, and the thought of being a sinner brought the illness which he believed was the inevitable consequence of sin. The first thing that Jesus said to him

was, 'Child, God is not angry with you. It's all right.' It was
like speaking to a frightened child in the dark. The burden
of the terror of God and estrangement from God rolled from
his heart, and that very fact made the cure all but complete.

It is a lovely story because the first thing that Jesus does
for every one of us is to say, 'Child, God is not angry with
you. Come home, and don't be afraid.'

Love and law

Matthew 12:9–14

He left there and went into their synagogue. And, look you, there was a man there with a withered hand. So they asked him: 'Is it permitted to heal on the Sabbath?' They asked this question in order that they might find an accusation against him. 'What man will there be of you', he said, 'who will have a sheep, and, if the sheep falls into a pit on the Sabbath day, will not take a grip of it, and lift it out? How much more valuable is a man than a sheep? So, then, it is permitted to do a good thing on the Sabbath day.' Then he said to the man: 'Stretch forth your hand!' He stretched it out, and it was restored, sound as the other. So the Pharisees went away and conferred against him, to find a way to destroy him.

This incident is a crucial moment in the life of Jesus. He deliberately and publicly broke the Sabbath law. The law quite definitely forbade healing on the Sabbath. It was true that the law clearly laid it down that 'every case when life is in danger supersedes the Sabbath law'. This was particularly the case in diseases of the ear, the nose, the throat and the eyes. But even then it was equally clearly laid down that steps could be taken to keep the sick or injured from getting worse, but not to make them better. So a plain bandage might be put on a wound, but not a medicated bandage, and so on.

In this case, there was no question of the paralysed man's life being in danger; as far as danger went, he would be in no worse condition the next day. Jesus knew the law; he knew what he was doing; he knew that the Pharisees were waiting and watching; *and yet he healed the man*. Jesus would accept no law which insisted that people should suffer, even without danger to life, one moment longer than necessary. His love for humanity far surpassed his respect for ritual law.

The challenge accepted

Matthew 12:9–14 (*contd*)

JESUS went into the synagogue, and in it was a man with a paralysed hand. Our gospels tell us nothing more about this man; but the Gospel according to the Hebrews, which was one of the early gospels which did not succeed in gaining an entry to the New Testament, tells us that he came to Jesus with the appeal: 'I was a stone mason, seeking my living with my hands. I pray you, Jesus, to give me back my health, so that I shall not need to beg for food in shame.'

But the scribes and Pharisees were there, too. They were not concerned with the man with the paralysed hand; they were concerned only with the minutest details of their rules and regulations. So they asked Jesus: 'Is it permitted to heal on the Sabbath day?' Jesus knew the answer to that question perfectly well; he knew that, as we have seen, unless there was actual danger to life, healing was forbidden, because it was regarded as an act of work.

But Jesus was wise. If they wished to argue about the law, he had the skill to meet them on their own ground. 'Tell me,' he said, 'suppose a man has a sheep, and that sheep falls into a pit on the Sabbath day, will he not go and haul the sheep out of the pit?' That was, in fact, a case for which the law provided. If an animal fell into a pit on the Sabbath, then it was within the law to carry food to it, which in any other case would have been a burden, and to help it in any way possible. 'So,' said Jesus, 'it is permitted to do a good thing on the Sabbath; and, if it is permitted to do a good thing to a sheep, how much more must it be lawful to do it for a man, who is of so much more value than any animal?'

Jesus reversed the argument. 'If', he argued, 'it is right to do good on the Sabbath, then to refuse to do good is evil.' It was Jesus' basic principle that there is no time so sacred that it cannot be used for helping someone who is in need. We will not be judged by the number of church services we have attended, or by the number of chapters of the Bible we have read, or even by the number of the hours we have spent in prayer, but by the number of people we have helped, when their need came crying to us. To this, at the moment, the scribes and Pharisees had nothing to answer, for their argument had rebounded on them.

So Jesus healed this man, and in healing him gave him three things.

(1) He gave him back his *health*. Jesus is vitally interested in people's physical wellbeing. Paul Tournier, in his book *A Doctor's Case Book*, has some great things to pass on about healing and God. Professor Courvoisier writes that the

vocation of medicine is 'a service to which those are called, who, through their studies and the natural gifts with which the Creator has endowed them … are specially fitted to tend the sick and to heal them. Whether or not they are aware of it, whether or not they are believers, this is from the Christian point of view fundamental, that doctors are, by their profession, fellow-workers with God.' 'Sickness and healing', said Dr Pouyanne, 'are acts of grace.' 'The doctor is an instrument of God's patience,' writes Pastor Alain Perrot. 'Medicine is a dispensation of the grace of God, who in his goodness takes pity on men and provides remedies for the evil consequences of their sin.' John Calvin described medicine as a gift from God. Those who bring healing are helping God. The cure of human bodies is just as much a God-given task as the cure of their souls; and doctors in general practice are just as much servants of God as ministers in parishes.

(2) Because Jesus gave this man back his health, he also gave him back his *work*. Without work to do, many people feel incomplete, because it is in their work that they find satisfaction and discover a real sense of identity. Over the years, idleness can be harder than pain to bear; and, if there is work to do, even sorrow loses at least something of its bitterness. One of the greatest things that any human being can do for others is to give them work to do.

(3) Because Jesus gave this man back his health and his work, he gave him back his *self-respect*. We might well add a new beatitude: blessed are those who give us back our self-respect. We discover our own worth again when, on our two feet and with our own two hands, we can face life and, with independence, provide for our own needs and for the needs of those dependent on us.

We have already said that this incident was a critical moment. At the end of it, the scribes and Pharisees began to plot the death of Jesus. In a sense, the highest compliment you can pay people is to persecute them. It shows that they are regarded not only as dangerous but also as effective. The action of the scribes and Pharisees is the measure of the power of Jesus Christ. True Christianity may be hated, but it can never be disregarded.

A private miracle

Mark 1:29–31

> *And immediately, when they had come out of the synagogue, they went, along with Peter and John, into the house of Simon and Andrew. Peter's mother-in-law was in bed with an attack of fever. Immediately they spoke to Jesus about her. He went up to her and took her by the hand and raised her up, and the fever left her, and she attended to their needs.*

THE synagogue service ended and Jesus went with his friends to Peter's house. According to Jewish custom the main Sabbath meal came immediately after the synagogue service, at the sixth hour, that is at 12 noon. (The Jewish day began at 6 am and the hours are counted from then.) Jesus might well have claimed the right to rest after the exciting and exhausting experience of the synagogue service; but once again his power was appealed to and once again he gave of himself for others. This miracle tells us something about three people.

(1) It tells us something about *Jesus*. He did not require an audience in order to exert his power; he was just as prepared to heal in the little circle of a cottage as in the great crowd of a synagogue. He was never too tired to help; the need of others took precedence over his own desire for rest. But above all, we see here, as we saw in the synagogue, the uniqueness

of the methods of Jesus. There were many exorcists in the time of Jesus, but they worked with elaborate incantations, and formulae, and spells, and magical apparatus. In the synagogue, Jesus had spoken one authoritative sentence and the healing was complete.

Here we have the same thing again. Peter's mother-in-law was suffering from what the Talmud called 'a burning fever'. It was, and still is, very prevalent in that particular part of Galilee. The Talmud actually lays down the methods of dealing with it. A knife entirely made of iron was tied by a braid of hair to a thorn bush. On successive days there was repeated, first, Exodus 3:2–3; second, Exodus 3:4; and finally Exodus 3:5. Then a certain magical formula was pronounced, and thus the cure was supposed to be achieved. Jesus completely disregarded all the paraphernalia of popular magic, and with a gesture and a word of unique authority and power he healed the woman.

The word that the Greek uses for authority in the previous passage is *exousia*; and *exousia* was defined as unique knowledge together with unique power; that is precisely what Jesus possessed, and that is what he was prepared to exercise in a cottage. Paul Tournier writes, 'My patients very often say to me, "I admire the patience with which you listen to everything I tell you." It is not patience at all, but interest.' A miracle to Jesus was not a means of increasing his prestige; to help was not a laborious and disagreeable duty; he helped instinctively, because he was supremely interested in all who needed his help.

(2) It tells us something about *the disciples*. They had not known Jesus long, but already they had begun to take all their troubles to him. Peter's mother-in-law was ill; the home was

upset; and it was for the disciples the most natural thing in the world to tell Jesus all about it.

Paul Tournier tells how one of life's greatest discoveries came to him. He used to visit an old Christian pastor who never let him go without praying with him. He was struck by the extreme simplicity of the old man's prayers. It seemed just a continuation of an intimate conversation that the old saint was always carrying on with Jesus. Tournier goes on, 'When I got back home I talked it over with my wife, and together we asked God to give us also the close fellowship with Jesus the old pastor had. Since then he has been the centre of my devotion and my travelling companion. He takes pleasure in what I do (cf. Ecclesiastes 9:7), and concerns himself with it. He is a friend with whom I can discuss everything that happens in my life. He shares my joy and my pain, my hopes and fears. He is there when a patient speaks to me from his heart, listening to him with me and better than I can. And when the patient is gone I can talk to him about it.'

Therein there lies the very essence of the Christian life. As the hymn has it, 'Take it to the Lord in prayer.' Thus early the disciples had learned what became the habit of a lifetime – to take all their troubles to Jesus and to ask his help for them.

(3) It tells us something about *Peter's wife's mother*. No sooner was she healed than she began to attend to their needs. She used her recovered health for renewed service. A great Scottish family has the motto 'Saved to Serve'. Jesus helps us that we may help others.

The peace of the presence

Mark 4:35–41

When on that day evening had come, he said to them, 'Let us cross over to the other side.' So they left the crowds and took him, just as he was, in their boat. And there were other boats with him. A great storm of wind got up and the waves dashed upon the boat, so that the boat was on the point of being swamped. And he was in the stern sleeping upon a pillow. They woke him. 'Teacher,' they said, 'don't you care that we are perishing?' So, when he had been wakened, he spoke sternly to the wind and said to the sea, 'Be silent! Be muzzled!' and the wind sank to rest and there was a great calm. He said to them, 'Why are you afraid? Have you still no faith?' And they were stricken with a great awe, and kept saying to each other, 'Who then can this be, because the wind and the sea obey him?'

THE Lake of Galilee was notorious for its storms. They came literally out of the blue with shattering and terrifying suddenness. A writer describes them like this: 'It is not unusual to see terrible squalls hurl themselves, even when the sky is perfectly clear, upon these waters which are ordinarily so calm. The numerous ravines which to the north-east and east debouch [open out] upon the upper part of the lake operate as so many dangerous defiles in which the winds from the heights of Hauran, the plateaux of Trachonitis, and the summit of Mount Hermon are caught and compressed in such a way that, rushing with tremendous force through a narrow space and then being suddenly released, they agitate the little Lake of Gennesaret in the most frightful fashion.' The voyager across the lake was always liable to encounter just such sudden storms as this.

Jesus was in the boat in the position in which any distinguished guest would be conveyed. We are told that, 'In these boats … the place for any distinguished stranger is on the little seat placed at the stern, where a carpet and cushion are arranged. The helmsman stands a little farther forward on the deck, though near the stern, in order to have a better look-out ahead.'

It is interesting to note that the words Jesus addressed to the wind and the waves are exactly the same as he addressed to the demon-possessed man in Mark 1:25. Just as an evil demon possessed that man, so the destructive power of the storm was, so people in Palestine believed in those days, the evil power of the demons at work in the realm of nature.

We do this story far less than justice if we merely take it in a literalistic sense. If it describes no more than a physical miracle in which an actual storm was stilled, it is very wonderful and it is something at which we must marvel, but it is something which happened once and cannot happen again. In that case it is quite external to us. But if we read it in a symbolic sense, it is far more valuable. When the disciples realized the presence of Jesus with them, the storm became a calm. Once they knew he was there, fearless peace entered their hearts. To voyage with Jesus was to voyage in peace even in a storm. Now that is universally true. It is not something which happened once; it is something which still happens and which can happen for us. In the presence of Jesus, we can have peace even in the wildest storms of life.

(1) He gives us peace in the storm of *sorrow*. When sorrow comes as come it must, he tells us of the glory of the life to come. He changes the darkness of death into the sunshine of the thought of life eternal. He tells us of the love of God. There is an old story of a gardener who in his garden had a favourite flower which he loved much. One day he came to the garden to find that flower gone. He was vexed and angry and full of complaints. In the midst of his resentment he met the master of the garden and hurled his complaints at him. 'Hush!' said the master, 'I plucked it for myself.' In the storm of sorrow Jesus tells us that those we love have gone to be with God, and gives us the certainty that we shall meet again those whom we have loved and lost awhile.

(2) He gives us peace when life's *problems* involve us in a tempest of doubt and tension and uncertainty. There come times when we do not know what to do; when we stand at some crossroads in life and do not know which way to take. If then we turn to Jesus and say to him, 'Lord, what will you have me to do?' the way will be clear. The real tragedy is not that we do not know what to do; but that often we do not humbly submit to Jesus' guidance. To ask his will and to submit to it is the way to peace at such a time.

(3) He gives us peace in the storms of *anxiety*. The chief enemy of peace is worry, worry for ourselves, worry about the unknown future, worry about those we love. But Jesus speaks to us of a Father whose hand will never cause his child a needless tear and of a love beyond which neither we nor those we love can ever drift. In the storm of anxiety, he brings us the peace of the love of God.

The defeat of the demons

Luke 8:26–39

They came in their voyage to the district of the Gerasenes, which is across the lake from Galilee. When Jesus had disembarked on the land there met him a man from the town who had demons. For a long time he had gone unclothed, and he did not stay in a house but among the tombs. When he saw Jesus he uttered a great cry and fell down before him and shouted, 'What have you and I to do with each other, Jesus, you Son of the Most High God? I beseech you – don't torture me!' – for Jesus had commanded the unclean spirit to come out of the man. For many a time it had snatched at him, and he was kept bound with chains and fetters, but when he was driven into the deserted places by the demons, he would burst the fetters. Jesus answered, 'What is your name?' He said, 'A regiment' – because many demons had entered into him, and they begged him not to order them to depart to the abyss. There was a herd of many pigs there, feeding on the mountainside. The demons asked him to allow them to go into them. He did so. So the demons came out of the man and into the pigs, and the herd rushed down the precipice into the lake and were drowned. When those who were in charge of them saw what had happened, they fled and brought the story to the town and to the countryside round about. They came out to see what had happened. They came to Jesus and found the

*man from whom the demons had gone out sitting there at
Jesus' feet, clothed and in his senses — and they were afraid.
Those who had seen what had happened told them how the
demon-possessed man had been cured; and the whole crowd
from the Gerasene countryside asked him to go away from
them, because they were in the grip of a great fear. So he
embarked on the ship and went away. The man from whom
the demons had gone out begged to be allowed to go with him;
but he sent him away. 'Go back,' he said, 'to your home and
tell the story of all that God did for you.' So he went away
and proclaimed throughout the whole town all that God had
done for him.*

WE will never even begin to understand this story unless
we realize that, whatever we think about the demons,
they were intensely real to the people of Gerasa and to the
man whose mind was deranged. This man was a case
of violent insanity. He was too dangerous to live in the
community and he lived amid the tombs, which were
believed to be the home and the haunt of demons. We may
well note the sheer courage of Jesus in dealing with him. The
man had a maniacal strength which enabled him to snap
his fetters. People were so terrified of him that they would
never try to do anything for him; but Jesus faced him calm
and unafraid.

When Jesus asked the man his name, he answered,
'Legion.' A Roman legion was a regiment of 6,000 soldiers.
Doubtless this man had seen a Roman legion on the march,
and his poor, afflicted mind felt that there was not one demon
but a whole regiment inside him. It may well be that the word
haunted him because he had seen atrocities carried out by a

Roman legion when he was a child. It is possible that it was the sight of such atrocities which left a scar upon his mind and ultimately caused his mental illness.

Far too much difficulty has been made out of the pigs. Jesus has been condemned for sending the demons into the innocent swine. That has been characterized as a cruel and immoral action. Again we must remember the intensity of the belief in demons. The man, thinking the demons were speaking through him, pleaded with Jesus not to send them into the abyss of hell to which they would be consigned in the final judgment. He would never have believed that he was cured unless he had visible demonstration. Nothing less than the visible departure of the demons would have convinced him.

Surely what happened was this. The herd of swine was feeding there on the mountainside. Jesus was exerting his power to cure what was a very stubborn case. Suddenly the man's wild shouts and screams disturbed the swine and they went dashing down the steep place into the sea in blind terror. 'Look!' said Jesus, 'Look! Your demons are gone!' Jesus *had* to find a way to get into the mind of this poor man; and in that way he found it.

In any event, can we compare the value of a herd of swine with the value of a man's immortal soul? If it cost the lives of these swine to save that soul, are we to complain? Is it not perverse fastidiousness which complains that swine were killed in order to heal a man? Surely we ought to preserve a sense of proportion. If the only way to convince this man of his cure was that the swine should perish, it seems quite extraordinarily blind to object that they did.

We must look at the reaction of two sets of people.

(1) There were *the Gerasenes*. They asked Jesus to go away.

(a) They hated having the routine of life disturbed. Life went peacefully on till there arrived this disturbing Jesus; and they hated him. More people hate Jesus because he disturbs them than for any other reason. If he says to someone, 'You must give up this habit, you must change your life'; if he says to an employer, 'You can't be a Christian and make people work under conditions like that'; if he says to a landlord, 'You can't take money for slums like that' – one and all are liable to say to him, 'Go away and let me be in peace.'

(b) They loved their swine more than they valued a human soul. One of life's supreme dangers is to value things more than persons. That is what created slums and vicious working conditions. Nearer home, that is what makes us selfishly demand our ease and comfort even if it means that someone who is tired has to slave for us. No thing in this world can ever be as important as a person.

(2) There was *the man who was cured*. Very naturally he wanted to come with Jesus but Jesus sent him home. Christian witness, like Christian charity, begins at home. It would be so much easier to live and speak for Christ among people who do not know us. But it is our duty, where Christ has set us, there to witness for him. And if it should happen that we are the only Christian in the shop, the office, the school, the factory, the circle in which we live or work, that is not a matter for lamentation. It is a challenge in which God says, 'Go and tell the people you meet every day what I have done for you.'

A soldier's faith

Luke 7:1–10

When Jesus had completed all his words in the hearing of the people, he went into Capernaum. The servant of a certain centurion was so ill that he was going to die, and he was very dear to him. When he heard about Jesus he sent some Jewish elders to him and asked him to come and save his servant's life. They came to Jesus and strenuously urged him to come. 'He is', they said, 'a man who deserves that you should do this for him, for he loves our nation and has himself built us our synagogue.' So Jesus went with them. When he was now quite near the house the centurion sent friends to him. 'Sir,' he said, 'do not trouble yourself. I am not worthy that you should come under my roof; nor do I count myself fit to come to you; but just speak a word and my servant will be cured. For I myself am a man under orders, and I have soldiers under me, and I say to one, "Go," and he goes; and to another, "Come," and he comes; and I say to my servant, "Do this," and he does it.' When Jesus heard this he was amazed at him. He turned to the crowd who were following him and said, 'I tell you I have not found such great faith not even in Israel.' And those who had been sent returned to the house and found the servant completely cured.

THE central character is a Roman centurion; and he was no ordinary man.

(1) The mere fact that *he was a centurion* meant he was no ordinary man. A centurion was the equivalent of a regimental sergeant-major; and the centurions were the backbone of the Roman army. Wherever they are spoken of in the New Testament they are spoken of well (cf. Luke 23:47; Acts 10:22; 22:26; 23:17, 23, 24; 24:23; 27:43). Polybius, the historian, describes their qualifications. They must be not so much 'seekers after danger as men who can command, steady in action, and reliable; they ought not to be over-anxious to rush into the fight; but when hard pressed they must be ready to hold their ground and die at their posts'. The centurion must have had the respect of his men or he would never have held the post which was his.

(2) *He had a completely unusual attitude to his slave.* He loved this slave and would go to any trouble to save him. In Roman law a slave was defined as a living tool; he had no rights; a master could ill-treat him and even kill him if he chose. A Roman writer on estate management recommends the farmer to examine his implements every year and to throw out those which are old and broken, and to do the same with his slaves. Normally when a slave was past his work he was thrown out to die. The attitude of this centurion to his slave was quite unusual.

(3) *He was clearly a deeply religious man.* A man would need to be more than superficially interested before he would go to the lengths of building a synagogue. It is true that the Romans encouraged religion from the cynical motive that it kept people in order. They regarded it as the opiate of the people. Augustus recommended the building of synagogues for that very reason. As Edward Gibbon, the author of *The Decline and Fall of the Roman Empire*, said in a famous

sentence, 'The various modes of religion which prevailed in the Roman world were all considered by the people as equally true; by the philosopher as equally false; *and by the magistrate as equally useful.*' But this centurion was no administrative cynic; he was a sincerely religious man.

(4) *He had an extremely unusual attitude to the Jews.* If the Jews despised the Gentiles, the Gentiles hated the Jews. Anti-semitism is not a new thing. The Romans called the Jews a filthy race; they spoke of Judaism as a barbarous superstition; they spoke of the Jewish hatred of humankind; they accused the Jews of worshipping an ass's head and annually sacrificing a Gentile stranger to their God. True, many of the Gentiles, weary of the many gods and loose morals of paganism, had accepted the Jewish doctrine of the one God and the austere Jewish ethic. But the whole atmosphere of this story implies a close bond of friendship between this centurion and the Jews.

(5) *He was a humble man.* He knew quite well that a strict Jew was forbidden by the law to enter the house of a Gentile (Acts 10:28); just as he was forbidden to allow a Gentile into his house or have any communication with him. He would not even come to Jesus himself. He persuaded his Jewish friends to approach him. This man who was accustomed to command had an amazing humility in the presence of true greatness.

(6) *He was a man of faith.* His faith is based on the soundest argument. He argued from the here and now to the there and then. He argued from his own experience to an understanding of God. If his authority produced the results it did, how much more must that of Jesus? He came with that perfect confidence which looks up and says, 'Lord, I know

you can do this.' If only we had a faith like that, for us too the miracle would happen and life become new.

The compassion of Christ

Luke 7:11–17

Next, after that, Jesus was on his way to a town called Nain; and his disciples and a great crowd accompanied him on the journey. When he came near the gate of the town – look you – a man who had died was being carried out to burial. He was his mother's only son, and she was a widow. There was a great crowd of townspeople with her. When the Lord saw her he was moved to the depths of his heart for her and said to her, 'Don't go on weeping!' He went up and touched the bier. Those who were carrying it stood still. 'Young man,' he said, 'I tell you, rise!' And the dead man sat up and began to speak. And he gave him back to his mother. And awe gripped them all. They glorified God saying, 'A great prophet has been raised up among us,' and, 'God has graciously visited his people.' This story about him went out in all Judaea and all the surrounding countryside.

IN this passage, as in the one immediately preceding, once again Luke the doctor speaks. In verse 10 the word we translated *completely cured* is the technical medical term for *sound in wind and limb*. In verse 15 the word used for *sitting up* is the technical term for a patient *sitting up in bed*.

Nain was a day's journey from Capernaum and lay between Endor and Shunem, where Elisha, as the old story runs, raised another mother's son (2 Kings 4:18–37). To this day, ten minutes' walk from Nain on the road to Endor there is a cemetery of rock tombs in which the dead are laid.

In many ways this is the loveliest story in all the gospels.

(1) It tells of *the pathos and the poignancy of human life*. The funeral procession would be headed by the band of professional mourners with their flutes and their cymbals, uttering in a kind of frenzy their shrill cries of grief. There is all the ageless sorrow of the world in the austere and simple sentence, 'He was his mother's only son, and she was a widow.'

> *Never morning wore to evening*
> *But some heart did break.*

In Shelley's *Adonais*, his lament for Keats, he writes:

> *As long as skies are blue, and fields are green,*
> *Evening must usher night, night urge the morrow,*
> *Month follow month with woe, and year wake*
> *   year to sorrow.*

Virgil, the Roman poet, in an immortal phrase spoke about 'The tears of things' – *sunt lacrimae rerum*. In the nature of things we live in a world of broken hearts.

(2) To the pathos of human life, Luke adds *the compassion of Christ*. Jesus was moved to the depths of his heart. There is no stronger word in the Greek language for sympathy and again and again in the gospel story it is used of Jesus (Matthew 14:14, 15:32, 20:34; Mark 1:41, 8:2).

To the ancient world this must have been a staggering thing. The noblest faith in antiquity was Stoicism. The Stoics believed that the primary characteristic of God was *apathy, incapability of feeling*. This was their argument. If someone can make another sad or sorry, glad or joyful, it means that, at least for the moment, he can influence that other person. If he can influence him that means that, at least for the moment, he is greater than the other person. Now, no one can be greater than God; therefore, no one can influence God; therefore, in the nature of things, God must be incapable of feeling.

Here we are presented with the amazing conception of one who was the Son of God being moved to the depths of his being. As Michael Bruce wrote:

> *In ev'ry pang that rends the heart,*
> *The Man of sorrows has a part.*

For many that is the most precious thing about the God and Father of our Lord Jesus Christ.

(3) To the compassion of Jesus, Luke adds *the power of Jesus*. He went up and touched the bier. It was not a coffin, for coffins were not used in the middle east. Very often long wickerwork baskets were used for carrying the body to the grave. It was a dramatic moment. In the words of one great commentator, 'Jesus claimed as his own what death had seized as his prey.'

It may well be that here we have a miracle of diagnosis; that Jesus with those keen eyes of his saw that the young man was in a cataleptic trance and saved him from being buried alive, as so many were in Palestine. It does not matter; the fact remains that Jesus claimed for life a young man who had been marked for death. Jesus is not only the Lord of life; he is the Lord of death who himself triumphed over the grave and who has promised that, because he lives, we shall live also (John 14:19).

The imperfect faith
and the perfect power

Matthew 9:18–31

BEFORE we deal with this passage in detail, we must look at it as a whole; for in it there is something wonderful.

It has three miracle stories in it: the healing of the ruler's daughter (verses 18–19, 23–6); the healing of the woman with the issue of blood (verses 20–2); and the healing of the two blind men (verses 27–31). Each of these stories has something in common. Let us look at them one by one.

(1) Beyond doubt, the ruler came to Jesus when everything else had failed. He was, as we shall see, a ruler of the synagogue; that is to say, he was a pillar of Jewish orthodoxy. He was one of the men who despised and hated Jesus, and who would have been glad to see him eliminated. No doubt he tried every kind of doctor, and every kind of cure; and only in sheer desperation, and as a last resort, did he come to Jesus at all.

That is to say, *the ruler came to Jesus from a very inadequate motive*. He did not come to Jesus as a result of an outflow of the love of his heart; he came to Jesus because he had tried everything and everyone else, and because there was nowhere else to go. The hymn-writer F. W. Faber makes God say of a straying child of God:

> *If goodness lead him not,*
> *Then weariness may toss him to my breast.*

This man came to Jesus simply because desperation drove him there.

(2) The woman with the issue of blood crept up behind Jesus in the crowd and touched the hem of his cloak. Suppose we were reading that story with a detached and critical awareness, what would we say that woman showed? We would say that she showed nothing other than superstition. To touch the edge of Jesus' cloak is the same kind of thing as to look for healing power in the relics and the handkerchiefs of saints.

This woman came to Jesus with what we would call a very inadequate faith. She came with what seems much more like superstition than faith.

(3) The two blind men came to Jesus, crying out: 'Have pity on us, you Son of David.' *Son of David* was not a title that Jesus desired; *Son of David* was the kind of title that a Jewish nationalist might use. So many of the Jews were waiting for a great leader of the line of David who would be the conquering general who would lead them to military and political triumph over their Roman masters. That is the idea which lies behind the title *Son of David*.

So *these blind men came to Jesus with a very inadequate conception of who he was.* They saw in him no more than the conquering hero of David's line.

Here is an astonishing thing. The ruler came to Jesus with an *inadequate motive*; the woman came to Jesus with an *inadequate faith*; the blind men came to Jesus with an *inadequate conception* of who he was, or, if we like to put it so, with an *inadequate theology*; and yet they found his love and power waiting for their needs. Here we see a tremendous thing. It does not matter how we come to Christ, if only we come. No matter how inadequately and how imperfectly we come, his love and his arms are open to receive us.

There is a double lesson here. It means that we do not wait to ask Christ's help until our motives, our faith and our theology are perfect; we may come to him exactly as we are. And it means that we have no right to criticize others whose motives we suspect, whose faith we question and whose theology we believe to be mistaken. It is not how we come to Christ that matters; it is that we should come at all, for he is willing to accept us as we are, and able to make us what we ought to be.

The awakening touch

Matthew 9:18–19, 23–6

> *While he was saying these things, look you, a ruler came and knelt before him in worship. 'My daughter', he said, 'has just died. But come and lay your hand upon her, and she will live.' Jesus rose and went with him, and his disciples came too … And Jesus came to the house of the ruler, and he saw the flute-players and the tumult of the crowd. 'Leave us,' he said, 'for the maid is not dead; she is asleep.' And they laughed at him. When the crowd had been put out, he went in and took*

her hand, and the maid arose. And the report of this went out
to the whole country.

MATTHEW tells this story much more briefly than the other gospel writers do. If we want further details of it, we must read it in Mark 5:21–43 and in Luke 8:40–56. There we discover that the ruler's name was Jairus, and that he was a ruler of the synagogue (Mark 5:22; Luke 8:41).

The ruler of the synagogue was a very important person. He was elected from among the elders. He was not a teaching or a preaching official; he had 'the care of the external order in public worship, and the supervision of the concerns of the synagogue in general'. He appointed those who were to read and to pray in the service, and invited those who were to preach. It was his duty to see that nothing unfitting took place within the synagogue; and the care of the synagogue buildings was in his oversight. The whole practical administration of the synagogue was in his hands.

It is clear that such a man would come to Jesus only as a last resort. He would be one of those strictly orthodox Jews who regarded Jesus as a dangerous heretic; and it was only when everything else had failed that he turned in desperation to Jesus. Jesus might well have said to him: 'When things were going well with you, you wanted to kill me; now that things are going badly, you are appealing for my help.' And Jesus might well have refused help to a man who came like that. But he bore no grudge; here was a man who needed him, and Jesus' one desire was to help. Injured pride and the unforgiving spirit had no part in the mind of Jesus.

So Jesus went with the ruler of the synagogue to his house, and there he found a scene of pandemonium. The

Jews set very high the obligation of mourning over the dead. 'Whoever is remiss', they said, 'in mourning over the death of a wise man deserves to be burned alive.' There were three mourning customs which characterized every Jewish household of grief.

There was the *rending of garments*. There were no fewer than thirty-nine different rules and regulations which laid down how garments should be rent. The rent was to be made standing. Clothes were to be rent to the heart so that the skin was exposed. For a father or mother, the rent was exactly over the heart; for others, it was on the right side. The rent must be big enough for a fist to be inserted into it. For seven days, the rent must be left gaping open; for the next thirty days, it must be loosely stitched so that it could still be seen; only then could it be permanently repaired. It would obviously have been improper for women to rend their garments in such a way that the breast was exposed. So it was laid down that a woman must rend her inner garment in private; she must then reverse the garment so that she wore it back to front; and then in public she must rend her outer garment.

There was *wailing for the dead*. In a house of grief, an incessant wailing was kept up. The wailing was done by professional wailing women. They still exist in the middle east, and W. M. Thomson in *The Land and the Book* describes them: 'There are in every city and community women exceedingly cunning in this business. They are always sent for and kept in readiness. When a fresh company of sympathisers comes in, these women make haste to take up a wailing, that the newly-come may the more easily unite their tears with the mourners. They know the domestic history of every person, and immediately strike up an impromptu lamentation, in which they introduce the names of their relatives who have recently died, touching some tender chord in every heart; and thus each one weeps for his own dead, and the performance, which would otherwise be difficult or impossible, comes easy and natural.'

There were *the flute-players*. The music of the flute was especially associated with death. The *Talmud* lays it down: 'The husband is bound to bury his dead wife, and to make lamentations and mourning for her, according to the custom of all countries. And also the very poorest among the Israelites will not allow her less than two flutes and one wailing woman; but, if he be rich, let all things be done according to his qualities.' Even in Rome, the flute-players were a feature of days of grief. There were flute-players at the funeral of the Roman emperor Claudius, and Seneca tells us that they made such a shrilling that even Claudius himself, dead though he was, might have heard them. So insistent and so emotionally exciting was the wailing of the flute that Roman law limited the number of flute-players at any funeral to ten.

We can then picture the scene in the house of the ruler of the synagogue. The garments were being torn; the wailing women were uttering their shrieks in an abandonment of synthetic grief; the flutes were shrilling their eerie sound. In that house, there was all the pandemonium of middle-eastern grief.

Into that excited and hysterical atmosphere came Jesus. Authoritatively he sent them all out. Quietly he told them that the girl was not dead but only asleep, and they laughed at him. It is a strangely human touch, this. The mourners were so luxuriating in their grief that they even resented hope.

It is probable that when Jesus said the girl was asleep, he meant exactly what he said. In Greek as in English, a dead person was often said to be asleep. In fact, the word cemetery comes from the Greek word *koimētērion* and means *a place where people sleep*. In Greek there are two words for *to sleep*: the one is *koimasthai*, which is very commonly used both of natural sleep and of the sleep of death; the other is *katheudein*, which is not used nearly so frequently of the sleep of death, but which much more usually means natural sleep. It is *katheudein* which is used in this passage.

In this part of the world, cataleptic coma was by no means uncommon. Burial in the middle east follows death very quickly, because the climate makes it necessary. Henry Baker Tristram, who travelled extensively in the Bible lands, writes: 'Interments always take place at latest on the evening of the day of death, and frequently at night, if the deceased have lived till after sunset.' Because of the commonness of this state of coma, and because of the commonness of speedy burial, not infrequently people were buried alive, as the evidence of the tombs shows. It may well be that here we have an example not so much of divine healing as of divine diagnosis; and that Jesus saved this girl from a terrible end.

One thing is certain: Jesus that day in Capernaum rescued a young Jewish girl from the grasp of death.

All heaven's power for one

Matthew 9:20–2

And, look you, a woman who had had a haemorrhage for twelve years came up behind him, and touched the tassel of his cloak. For she said to herself, 'If I only touch his cloak, I will be cured.' Jesus turned and saw her. 'Courage, daughter!' he said. 'Your faith has brought you healing.' And the woman was cured from that hour.

FROM the Jewish point of view, this woman could not have suffered from any more terrible or humiliating disease than an issue of blood. It was a trouble which was very common in Palestine. The *Talmud* sets out no fewer than eleven different cures for it. Some of them were tonics and astringents which may well have been effective; others were merely superstitious remedies. One was to carry the ashes of an ostrich egg in a linen bag in summer and in a cotton bag in winter; another was to carry about a barleycorn which had been found in the dung of a white she-ass. When Mark tells this story, he makes it clear that this woman had tried everything, and had gone to every available doctor, and was worse instead of better (Mark 5:26).

The horror of the disease was that it rendered the sufferer unclean. The law laid it down: 'If a woman has a discharge of blood for many days, not at the time of her impurity, or if she has a discharge beyond the time of her impurity, for all the days of the discharge she shall continue in uncleanness; as in the days of her impurity, she shall be unclean. Every bed on which she lies during all the days of her discharge

shall be treated as the bed of her impurity; and everything
on which she sits shall be unclean, as in the uncleanness of
her impurity. Whoever touches these things shall be unclean,
and shall wash his clothes, and bathe in water, and be unclean
until the evening' (Leviticus 15:25–7).

That is to say, a woman with an issue of blood was unclean;
everything and everyone she touched was infected with that
uncleanness. She was absolutely shut off from the worship
of God and from the fellowship of other men and women.
She should not even have been in the crowd surrounding
Jesus, for, if they had known it, she was infecting with her
uncleanness everyone whom she touched. There is little
wonder that she was desperately eager to try anything which
might rescue her from her life of isolation and humiliation.

So she slipped up behind Jesus and touched what the
Authorized Version calls the *hem* of his garment. The Greek
word is *kraspedon*, the Hebrew is *zizith*, and the Revised
Standard Version translates it as *fringe*.

These fringes were four tassels of hyacinth blue worn by
a Jew on the corners of his outer garment. They were worn in
obedience to the injunction of the law in Numbers 15:37–41
and Deuteronomy 22:12. Matthew again refers to them
in 14:36 and 23:5. They consisted of four threads passing
through the four corners of the garment and meeting in eight.
One of the threads was longer than the others. It was twisted
seven times round the others, and a double knot formed; then
eight times, then eleven times, then thirteen times. The thread
and the knots stood for the five books of the law.

The idea of the fringe was twofold. It was meant to
identify a Jew as a Jew, and as a member of the chosen people,
no matter where he was; and it was meant to remind a Jew

every time he put on and took off his clothes that he belonged to God. In later times, when the Jews were universally persecuted, the tassels were worn on the undergarment, and today they are worn on the prayer shawl which devout Jews wear when they pray.

It was the tassel on the robe of Jesus that this woman touched.

When she touched it, it was as if time stood still. It was as if we were watching a film and suddenly the picture stopped and left us looking at one scene. The extraordinary, and the movingly beautiful, thing about this scene is that all at once in the middle of that crowd Jesus halted; and for the moment it seemed that for him no one but that woman and nothing but her need existed. She was not simply a poor woman lost in the crowd; she was someone to whom Jesus gave the whole of himself.

For Jesus, no one is ever lost in the crowd, because Jesus is like God. The Irish poet W. B. Yeats once wrote in one of his moments of mystical beauty: 'The love of God is infinite for every human soul, because every human soul is unique; no other can satisfy the same need in God.' God gives all of himself to each individual person.

The world is not like that. The world is apt to divide people into those who are important and those who are unimportant. In *A Night to Remember*, Walter Lord tells in detail the story of the sinking of the *Titanic* in April 1912. There was an appalling loss of life when that new and supposedly unsinkable liner hit an iceberg in the middle of the Atlantic. After the tragedy had been announced, the New York newspaper *The American* featured a leading article devoted entirely to the death of John Jacob Astor, the millionaire; and at the end of the leader, almost casually, it was mentioned that 1,800 others were also lost. The only one who really mattered, the only one with real news value, was the millionaire. The other losses were of no real importance.

Men and women can be like that, but God can never be like that. Alexander Bain, the psychologist, said in a very different connection that the sensual person has what he calls 'a voluminous tenderness'. In the highest and the best sense, there is a voluminous tenderness in God. James Agate said of the writer G. K. Chesterton: 'Unlike some thinkers, Chesterton understood his fellow-men; the woes of a jockey were as familiar to him as the worries of a judge … Chesterton, more than any man I have ever known, had the common touch … He had about him that bounty of heart which men call kindness, and which makes the whole world kin.' That is the reflection of the love of God which does not allow anyone to be lost in the crowd.

This is something to remember in a day and an age when the individual is in danger of getting lost. Men and women tend to become numbers in a system of social security; they tend as members of an association or union almost to lose their right to be individuals at all. W. B. Yeats said of Augustus John, the famous artist and portrait painter: 'He was supremely interested in the revolt from all that makes one man like another.' To God, one person is never like another; each person is his individual child, and each of us has all God's love and all God's power at our disposal.

To Jesus, this woman was not lost in the crowd; in her hour of need, to him she was all that mattered. Jesus is like that for every one of us.

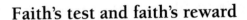

Faith's test and faith's reward

Matthew 9:27–31

> *And, as he passed on from there, two blind men followed him,*
> *shouting. 'Have pity on us,' they said, 'you Son of David.'*
> *When he came into the house, the blind men came to him.*
> *Jesus said to them, 'Do you believe that I am able to do this?'*
> *'Yes, Lord,' they said. Then he touched their eyes. 'Be it to you,'*
> *he said, 'according to your faith.' And their eyes were opened.*
> *And Jesus sternly commanded them, 'See, let no one know of*
> *this.' But they went out and spread abroad the story of him*
> *all over the country.*

BLINDNESS was a distressingly common disease in Palestine. It
came partly from the glare of the sun on unprotected eyes,
and partly because people knew nothing of the importance of
cleanliness and hygiene. In particular, the clouds of unclean
flies carried infections which led to loss of sight.

The name by which these two blind men addressed
Jesus was *Son of David*. When we study the occurrences of
that title within the gospels, we find that it is almost always
used by crowds or by people who knew Jesus only, as it
were, at a distance (Matthew 15:22, 20:30–1; Mark 10:47,
12:35–7). The term *Son of David* describes Jesus in the
popular conception of the Messiah. For centuries, the Jews
had awaited the promised deliverer of David's line, the leader
who would not only restore their freedom, but who would

lead them to power and glory and greatness. It was in that way that these blind men thought of Jesus; they saw in him the wonder-worker who would lead the people to freedom and to conquest. They came to Jesus with a very inadequate idea of who and what he was, and yet he healed them. The way in which Jesus dealt with them is illuminating.

(1) Clearly, he did not answer their shouts at once. Jesus wished to be quite sure that they were sincere and earnest in their desire for what he could give them. It might well have been that they had taken up a popular cry just because everyone else was shouting, and that, as soon as Jesus had passed by, they would simply forget. He wanted first of all to be sure that their request was genuine and that their sense of need was real.

After all, there were advantages in being a beggar; a man was rid of all the responsibility of working and of making a living.

There are people who in actual fact do not wish their chains to be broken. W. B. Yeats tells of Lionel Johnson, the scholar and poet. Johnson was an alcoholic. He had, as he said himself, 'a craving that made every atom of his body cry out'. But, when it was suggested that he should undergo treatment to overcome this craving, his answer quite frankly was: 'I do not want to be cured.'

There are not a few people who in their heart of hearts do not dislike their weakness; and there are many people who, if they were honest, would have to say that they do not wish to lose their sins. Jesus had first of all to be sure that these men sincerely and earnestly desired the healing he could give.

(2) It is interesting to note that Jesus in effect compelled these people to see him alone. Because he did not answer

them in the streets, they had to come to him in the house. It is the law of the spiritual life that sooner or later every individual must confront Jesus alone. It is all very well to take a decision for Jesus on the flood tide of emotion at some great gathering, or in some little group which is charged with spiritual power. But after the crowd, people have to go home and be alone; after the fellowship, they must go back to the essential isolation of every human soul; and what really matters is not what people do in the crowd, but what they do when they are alone with Christ. Jesus compelled these men to face him alone.

(3) Jesus asked these men only one question: 'Do you believe that I am able to do this?' The one essential for a miracle is faith. There is nothing mysterious or theological about this. No doctor can cure a sick person who goes to him in a completely hopeless frame of mind. No medicine will do any good if those taking it think they might as well be drinking water. The way to a miracle is to place one's life in the hands of Jesus Christ and say: 'I know that you can make me what I ought to be.'

Light for the blind eyes

John 9:1–5

> As Jesus was passing by, he saw a man who was blind from the
> day of his birth. 'Rabbi,' his disciples said to him, 'who was it
> who sinned that he was born blind – this man or his parents?'
> 'It was neither he nor his parents who sinned,' answered Jesus,
> 'but it happened that in him there might be a demonstration
> of what God can do. We must do the works of him who sent
> me while day lasts; the night is coming when no man is able to
> work. So long as I am in the world, I am the light of the world.'

THIS is the only miracle in the gospels in which the sufferer
is said to have been afflicted from his birth. In Acts, we twice
hear of people who had been helpless from their birth (the
lame man at the Beautiful Gate of the Temple in Acts 3:2,
and the cripple at Lystra in Acts 14:8), but this is the only
man in the gospel story who had been so afflicted. He must
have been a well-known character, for the disciples knew
all about him.

When they saw him, they used the opportunity to put to
Jesus a problem with which Jewish thought had always been
deeply concerned, and which is still a problem. The Jews
connected suffering and sin. They worked on the assumption
that wherever there was suffering, somewhere there was sin.
So they asked Jesus their question. 'This man', they said, 'is

blind. Is his blindness due to his own sin, or to the sin of his parents?'

How could the blindness possibly be due to his own sin, when he had been blind *from his birth*? To that question, the Jewish theologians gave two answers.

(1) Some of them had the strange notion of pre-natal sin. They actually believed that it was possible to begin to sin while still in the womb. In the imaginary conversations between Antoninus and Rabbi Judah the Patriarch, Antoninus asks: 'From what time does the evil influence bear sway over a man, from the formation of the embryo in the womb or from the moment of birth?' The Rabbi first answered: 'From the formation of the embryo.' Antoninus disagreed and convinced Judah by his arguments, for Judah admitted that, if the evil impulse began with the formation of the embryo, then the child would kick in the womb and break his way out. Judah found a text to support this view. He took the saying in Genesis 4:7: 'Sin is lurking at the door.' And he put the meaning into it that sin awaited human life at the door of the womb, as soon as a child was born. But the argument does show us that the idea of pre-natal sin was known.

(2) In the time of Jesus, the Jews believed in the pre-existence of the soul. They really got that idea from Plato and the Greeks. They believed that all souls existed before the creation of the world in the garden of Eden, or that they were in the seventh heaven, or in a certain chamber, waiting to enter into a body. The Greeks had believed that such souls were good, and that it was the entry into the body which contaminated them; but there were certain Jews who believed that these souls were already good and bad. The writer of The Book of Wisdom says: 'As a

child I was naturally gifted, and a good soul fell to my lot' (Wisdom 8:19).

In the time of Jesus, certain Jews did believe that a person's affliction, even if it was from birth, might come from sin that had been committed before that person was born. It is a strange idea, and it may seem to us almost fantastic; but at its heart lies the idea of a sin-infected universe.

The alternative was that this man's affliction was due to the sin of his parents. The idea that children inherit the consequences of their parents' sin is woven into the thought of the Old Testament. 'I the Lord your God am a jealous God, punishing the children for the iniquity of parents, to the third and the fourth generation' (Exodus 20:5; cf. Exodus 34:7; Numbers 14:18). Of the wicked man, the psalmist says: 'May the iniquity of his father be remembered before the Lord, and do not let the sin of his mother be blotted out' (Psalm 109:14). Isaiah talks about their iniquities and 'their ancestors' iniquities', and goes on to say: 'I will measure into their laps full payment for their actions' (Isaiah 65:7). One of the keynotes of the Old Testament is that the sins of the parents are always visited upon the children. It must never be forgotten that we do not live in isolation from others and we do not die in isolation from others. When we sin, we set in motion a train of consequences which has no end.

In this passage, there are two great eternal principles.

(1) Jesus does not try to follow up or to explain the connection of sin and suffering. He says that this man's affliction came to him to give an opportunity of showing what God can do. There are two senses in which that is true.

(a) For John, the miracles are always a sign of the glory and the power of God. The writers of the other gospels had a different point of view, and regarded them as a demonstration of the compassion of Jesus. When Jesus looked on the hungry crowd he had *compassion* on them, because they were as sheep not having a shepherd (Mark 6:34). When the leper came with his desperate request for cleansing, Jesus was *moved with pity* (Mark 1:41). It is often urged that in this the Fourth Gospel is quite different from the others. Surely there is no real contradiction here. It is simply two ways of looking at the same thing. At its heart is the supreme truth that the glory of God lies in his compassion, and that he never so fully reveals his glory as when he reveals his pity.

(b) But there is another sense in which the man's suffering shows what God can do. Affliction, sorrow, pain, disappointment and loss are always opportunities for displaying God's grace. First, it enables the sufferer to show God in action. When trouble and disaster fall upon someone who does not know God, that person may well collapse; but when they fall on someone who walks with God, they bring out the strength and the beauty, and the endurance and the nobility, which are within a person's heart when God is there. It is told that when an old saint was dying in an agony of pain, he sent for his family, saying: 'Come and see how a Christian can die.' It is when life hits us a terrible blow that we can show the world how a Christian can live, and, if need be, die. Any kind of suffering is an opportunity to demonstrate the glory of God in our own lives. Second, by helping those who are in trouble or in pain, we can demonstrate to others the glory of God. The American missionary Frank Laubach has the great thought that when

Christ, who is the Way, enters into us, 'we become part of the Way. God's highway runs straight through us.' When we spend ourselves to help those in trouble, in distress, in pain, in sorrow, in affliction, God is using us as the highway by which he sends his help into the lives of his people. To help another person in need is to manifest the glory of God, for it is to show what God is like.

(2) Jesus goes on to say that he and all his followers must do God's work while there is time to do it. God gave the day for work and the night for rest; the day comes to an end, and the time for work is also ended. For Jesus, it was true that he had to press on with God's work in the day, for the night of the cross lay close ahead. But it is true for everyone. We are given only so much time. Whatever we are to do must be done within it. There is in Glasgow a sundial with the motto: 'Tak' tent of time ere time be tint.' 'Take thought of time before time is ended.' We should never put things off until another time, for another time may never come. Christians have a duty to fill the time they have – and no one knows how much that will be – with the service of God and of others. There is no more poignant sorrow than the tragic discovery that it is too late to do something which we might have done.

But there is another opportunity we may miss. Jesus said: 'So long as I am in the world, I am the light of the world.' When Jesus said that, he did not mean that the time of his life and work were limited but that our opportunity of laying hold on him is limited. There comes to each one of us a chance to accept Christ as our Saviour, our Master and our Lord; and if that opportunity is not seized it may well never come back. E. D. Starbuck in *The Psychology of Religion* has some interesting and warning statistics about the age at which conversion normally occurs. It can occur as early as seven or eight; it increases gradually to the age of ten or eleven; it increases rapidly to the age of sixteen; it declines steeply up to the age of twenty; and after thirty it is very rare. God is always saying to us: 'Now is the time.' It is not that the power of Jesus grows less, or that his light grows dim; it is that if we put off the great decision we become increasingly less able to take it as the years go on. Work must be done, decisions must be taken, while it is day, before the night falls.

The method of a miracle

John 9:6–12

> When he had said this he spat on the ground, and made clay from the spittle, and he smeared the clay on his eyes and said to him: 'Go, wash in the Pool of Siloam.' (The word 'Siloam' means 'sent'.) So he went away and washed, and he came able to see. So the neighbours and those who formerly knew him by sight and knew that he was a beggar, said: 'Is this not the man who sat begging?' Some said: 'It is he.' Others said: 'It is not he, but it is someone like him.' The man himself said: 'I am he.' 'How then', they said to him, 'have your eyes been opened?' 'The man they call Jesus made clay,' he said, 'and smeared it on my eyes, and said to me: "Go to the Pool of Siloam and wash." So I went and washed, and sight came

to me.' They said to him: 'Where is this man you are talking about?' He said: 'I don't know.'

THIS is one of two miracles in which Jesus is said to have used spittle to effect a cure. The other is the miracle of the deaf stammerer (Mark 7:33). The use of spittle seems to us strange and repulsive and unhygienic; but in the ancient world it was quite common. Spittle, and especially the spittle of some distinguished person, was believed to possess certain curative qualities. Tacitus tells how, when the Roman emperor Vespasian visited Alexandria, there came to him two men, one with diseased eyes and one with a diseased hand, who said that they had been advised by their god to come to him. The man with the diseased eyes wished Vespasian 'to moisten his eye-balls with spittle'; the man with the diseased hand wished Vespasian 'to trample on his hand with the sole of his foot'. Vespasian was very unwilling to do so but was finally persuaded to do as the men asked. 'The hand immediately recovered its power; the blind man saw once more. Both facts are attested to this day, when falsehood can bring no reward, by those who were present on the occasion' (Tacitus, *Histories*, 4:81).

Pliny, the famous Roman collector of what was then called scientific information, has a whole chapter on the use of spittle. He says that it is a sovereign preservative against the poison of serpents; that it is a protection against epilepsy; that lichens and leprous spots can be cured by the application of fasting spittle; that ophthalmia can be cured by anointing the eyes every morning with fasting spittle; that carcinomata and crick in the neck can be cured by the use of spittle. Spittle was held to be very effective in averting the evil eye. Persius tells how the aunt or the grandmother, who fears the gods and is skilled in averting the evil eye, will lift the baby from his cradle and 'with her middle finger apply the lustrous spittle to his forehead and slobbering lips'. The use of spittle was very common in the ancient world. To this day, if we burn a finger, our first instinct is to put it into our mouth; and there are some who believe that warts can be cured by licking them with fasting spittle.

The fact is that Jesus took the methods and customs of his time and used them. He was a wise physician; he had to gain the confidence of his patient. It was not that he believed in these things, but he kindled expectation by doing what the patient would expect a doctor to do. After all, to this day the efficacy of any medicine or treatment depends to a certain extent on the patient's faith in it as well as in the treatment or the drug itself.

After anointing the man's eyes with spittle, Jesus sent him to wash in the Pool of Siloam. The Pool of Siloam was one of the landmarks of Jerusalem; and it was the result of one of the great engineering feats of the ancient world. The water supply of Jerusalem had always been precarious in the event of a siege. It came mainly from the Virgin's Fountain or the Spring Gihon, which was situated in the Kedron Valley. A staircase of thirty-three rock-cut steps led down to it; and there, from a stone basin, people drew the water. But the spring was completely exposed and, in the event of a siege, could be completely cut off, with disastrous consequences.

When Hezekiah realized that Sennacherib was about to invade Palestine, he determined to cut through the solid rock a tunnel or conduit from the spring into the city (2 Chronicles

32:2–8, 30; Isaiah 22:9–11; 2 Kings 20:20). If the engineers had cut straight, it would have been a distance of 366 yards; but because they cut in a zig-zag, either because they were following a fissure in the rock, or to avoid sacred sites, the conduit is actually 583 yards long. The tunnel is in places only about two feet wide, but its average height is about six feet. The engineers began their cutting from both ends and met in the middle – a truly amazing feat for the equipment of the time.

In 1880, a tablet was discovered commemorating the completion of the conduit. It was accidentally discovered by two boys who were wading in the pool. It runs like this: 'The boring through is completed. Now is the story of the boring through. While the workmen were still lifting pick to pick, each towards his neighbour, and while three cubits remained to be cut through, each heard the voice of the other who called his neighbour, since there was a crevice in the rock on the right side. And on the day of the boring through the stone-cutters struck, each to meet his fellow, pick to pick; and there flowed the waters to the pool for 1,200 cubits, and 100 cubits was the height of the rock above the heads of the stone-cutters.'

The Pool of Siloam was the place where the conduit from the Virgin's Fountain issued in the city. It was an open-air basin twenty by thirty feet across. That is how the pool got its name. It was called *Siloam*, which, it was said, meant *sent*, because the water in it had been *sent* through the conduit into the city. Jesus sent this man to wash in this pool; and the man washed and saw.

Having been cured, he had some difficulty in persuading the people that a real cure had been effected. But he stoutly maintained the miracle which Jesus had performed. Jesus is still doing things which seem to the unbeliever far too good and far too wonderful to be true.

A notable deed is done

Acts 3:1–10

Peter and John used to go up to the Temple at the hour of prayer at 3 pm; and a man who had been lame from the day of his birth was in the habit of being carried there. Every day, they used to put him at the gate of the Temple which is called the Beautiful Gate, so that he could beg for alms from the people who were going into the Temple. When he saw Peter and John about to go into the Temple, he asked to be given alms. Peter fixed his eyes on him with John and said: 'Look at us.' He paid attention to them because he was expecting to get something from them. Peter said to him: 'Silver and gold I do not possess, but what I have I give you. In the name of Jesus Christ of Nazareth – walk!' And he took him by the right hand and lifted him up. Immediately his feet and ankle bones were strengthened, and he leaped up and stood and walked about; and he went into the Temple with them, walking about and leaping and praising God. Everyone saw him walking about and praising God; and they recognized him as the man who had sat at the Beautiful Gate of the Temple to receive alms. They were filled with amazement and astonishment at what had happened to him.

THE Jewish day began at 6 am and ended at 6 pm. For devout Jews, there were three special times for prayer –

morning, noon and evening. They agreed that prayer was effective wherever it was offered, but they felt that it was doubly precious when offered in the Temple courts. It is very interesting that the apostles kept up the customs in which they had been trained. It was the hour of prayer, and Peter and John were going into the Temple to observe it. A new faith had come to them, but they did not use that as an excuse to break the old law. They were aware that the new faith and the old discipline could walk hand in hand.

In the middle east, it was the custom for beggars to sit at the entrance to a temple or a shrine. Such a place was considered the best of all positions because, when people are on their way to worship God, they are disposed to be generous to others. W. H. Davies, the tramp poet, tells how one of his vagrant friends told him that, whenever he came into a new town, he looked for a church spire with a cross on the top and began to beg in that area. Love of other people and love of God must always go hand in hand.

This incident brings us face to face with the question of miracles in the apostolic times. There are certain definite things to be said.

(1) Such miracles *did* happen. In Acts 4:16, we read how the Sanhedrin knew that they must accept the miracle. The enemies of Christianity would have been the first to deny miracles if they could; but they never even try to deny them.

(2) Why did they stop? Certain suggestions have been made.

(a) There was a time when miracles were necessary. In that period, they were needed as a guarantee of the truth and the power of the Christian message in its initial attack on the world.

(b) At that time, two special circumstances came together. First, there were still those among the apostles who had had personal contact with Jesus Christ, which could never be repeated. Second, there was an atmosphere of expectancy when faith was in full flow. These two things combined to produce effects which were unique.

(3) The real question is not 'Why have miracles stopped?' but 'Have they stopped?' It is the simple fact that any doctor or surgeon can now do things which in apostolic times would have been regarded as miracles. God has revealed new truth and new knowledge to us, and through that revelation they are still performing miracles. As a great doctor said, 'I bandage the wounds; but God heals them.' For Christians, there are still miracles all around if they have eyes to see.

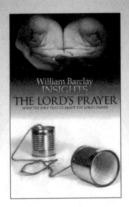

Christmas

What the Bible Tells Us about the Christmas Story

WILLIAM BARCLAY

Foreword by
NICK BAINES

978-0-7152-0858-8 (paperback)

See our website for details.
www.standrewpress

SAINT ANDREW PRESS

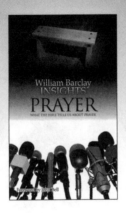

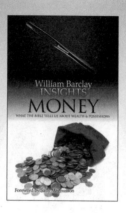

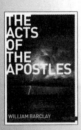  

Books by
WILLIAM BARCLAY

INSIGHTS SERIES

The Lord's Prayer
Christmas
Easter
Money
Prayer
Joy
Parables
Miracles

THE NEW DAILY STUDY BIBLE

The Gospel of Matthew Vol. 1
The Gospel of Matthew Vol. 2
The Gospel of Mark
The Gospel of Luke
The Gospel of John Vol. 1
The Gospel of John Vol. 2
The Acts of the Apostles
The Letter to the Romans
The Letters to the Corinthians
The Letters to the Galatians and the Ephesians
The Letters to the Philippians, Colossians and Thessalonians
The Letters to Timothy, Titus and Philemon
The Letter to the Hebrews
The Letters to James and Peter
The Letters of John and Jude
The Revelation of John Vol. 1
The Revelation of John Vol. 2

MISCELLANEOUS

A Beginner's Guide to the New Testament
God's Young Church